Building

Christian English

Building Securely

Grade 7

Tests

Rod and Staff Publishers, Inc.
Hwy. 172, Crockett, Kentucky 41413
Telephone: (606) 522-4348

by

Rod and Staff Publishers, Inc.

Hwy. 172, Crockett, Kentucky 41413

Printed in U.S.A

ISBN 978-07399-0530-2

Catalog no. 12717.3

12 13 14 15 — 23 22 21 20 19 18 17 16

Building Securely

Chapter 1 Test

Score ____________

Name ____ **Date** ________________________

A. Circle *T* if the statement is true or *F* if it is false.

T F 1. Every sentence must have a subject and a predicate.

T F 2. A fragment may contain a skeleton.

T F 3. An object complement may follow a linking verb.

T F 4. An indirect object is found right after a direct object.

T F 5. In a sentence containing a predicate adjective, the verb is much like an equal sign.

T F 6. Subjective complements include predicate nominatives and predicate adjectives.

T F 7. A good character sketch describes several outstanding characteristics of a person.

T F 8. It is usually best to proofread your story as soon as you have finished writing it.

(8 points)

B. Match the terms to the descriptions by writing the letter of the correct choice in the blank. Each set has one choice that you will not use.

_____ 9. Word group without a complete thought.

_____ 10. Tells *who* or *what* a sentence is about.

_____ 11. Two or more sentences joined incorrectly.

_____ 12. Tells what the subject *does* or *is*.

_____ 13. Completes the sentence skeleton.

a. complement
b. fragment
c. predicate
d. run-on error
e. skeleton
f. subject

_____ 14. Receives the action of a verb.

_____ 15. Modifies the subject.

_____ 16. Names the person to whom one is speaking.

_____ 17. Tells *to whom or what* or *for whom or what* an action is performed.

_____ 18. Renames the subject.

_____ 19. Immediately follows a noun or pronoun to identify or explain it.

g. appositive
h. direct object
i. indirect object
j. simple predicate
k. predicate adjective
l. predicate nominative
m. noun of direct address

(11 points)

C. Label each item *S* for sentence, *F* for fragment, or *R* for run-on error.

______ 20. Because the weather was beautiful.

______ 21. We took a walk through the woods.

______ 22. Which cover about twenty acres.

______ 23. A rabbit darted across the trail Spotty almost caught it.

(4 points)

D. Draw a vertical line to show the division between the complete subject and the complete predicate. Underline each simple subject once and each simple predicate twice.

24. Man's early home was the Garden of Eden.

25. God talked to Adam and Eve in the cool of the evening.

26. The enemy of God came and tempted them.

27. Their sin against God brought fear into their hearts.

(12 points)

E. Underline the five direct objects and the four indirect objects. Identify each one by writing *DO* or *IO* above it.

28. Feed the chickens and gather the eggs.

29. Tell Gary the good news.

30. The Lord gives His people grace for each test.

31. Grandmother sent Linda and Lynette a post card.

(9 points)

F. Underline the two predicate nominatives and the three predicate adjectives. Identify each one by writing *PN* or *PA* above it.

32. Jesus is the King of Glory.

33. In His earthly ministry, He was meek and lowly.

34. In His death, He became the Lamb of sacrifice.

35. Now in heaven, He will remain highly exalted forever.

(5 points)

G. Underline the three nouns of direct address and the two appositives. Identify each one by writing *D* or *A* above it. Also add the missing commas.

36. "Lord thou hast been our dwelling place in all generations."

37. The Bible God's holy Word reveals to us the way of truth.

38. Stanley please read to us from 1 Corinthians 13 the Love Chapter.

39. Can you quote the Golden Rule Rosalie?

(5 points)

H. Diagram the skeletons and complements, and any appositive or noun of direct address.

40. James, please give your father this book.

41. This volume, a book about Bible customs, is a valuable reference tool.

42. The explanations are simple but thorough.

(13 points)

I. Find eight mistakes in these paragraphs. Show the necessary corrections by using the proper proofreading marks.

While Gideon was threshing weat by the winepress, God called him to deliver Israel. The angel said, "The Lord is with you." Gideon, distressed at Israel's bondage and slavery, replied, "If God with us, why are we so trubbled by the Midianites?"

To assure Gideon that the Lord with was him, the angel gave him a sine. When Gideon brought some food, the angel told him to put the meat and cakes on the rock and to pour out the broth. Then the angel touched the food with his staff. Fire came the rock and consumed all the food.

(8 points)

Total points: 75

Building Securely

Chapter 2 Test

Score ____________

Name ____ **Date** ______________________

A. Circle *T* if the statement is true or *F* if it is false.

T F 1. A comma is usually needed when inverted word order is used.

T F 2. A clause must contain both a subject and a predicate.

T F 3. A topic sentence should summarize the details of a paragraph.

T F 4. In a well-written paragraph, most of the sentences contain transitional words.

T F 5. An adjective clause usually begins with a relative pronoun.

T F 6. In using repetition of key words, it is wise to use synonyms.

(6 points)

B. Match the terms to the descriptions by writing the letters of the correct choices in the blanks. You may not use some choices in a set, and you may use some more than once.

a. declarative sentence
b. exclamatory sentence
c. imperative sentence
d. interrogative sentence

_____ 7. A sentence that expresses strong feeling.

_____ 8. A sentence that states a fact.

_____ 9. A sentence that asks a question.

_____ 10. A sentence that gives a command.

_____ 11. A sentence in which the subject is always *you*.

_____ 12. A sentence that often has special word order.

_____ 13. A sentence that must be either true or false.

e. inverted word order
f. mixed word order
g. natural word order

_____ 14. The complete predicate comes before the complete subject.

_____ 15. The complete subject comes before the complete predicate.

_____ 16. The complete subject comes between two parts of the predicate.

_____ 17. The word order that is most frequently used.

______	18. A sentence with only one independent clause.	h. complex sentence
______	19. A sentence with one independent clause and one or more dependent clauses.	i. compound sentence
______	20. A sentence with two or more independent clauses.	j. simple sentence
______	21. A sentence with clauses usually joined by a coordinating conjunction.	

______	22. Every sentence supports the main idea.	k. coherence
______	23. The first line is indented, and the margins are straight.	l. form
______	24. The sentences fit together smoothly.	m. topic sentence
		n. unity

______	25. Sentences arranged in the order of space.	o. chronological order
______	26. Sentences arranged in the order of time.	p. order of importance
______	27. The order used in describing a scene.	q. spatial order
______	28. The order used when several reasons are given to explain something.	
______	29. The order used in explaining a process.	

(23 points)

C. Label each sentence *dec.* (declarative), *int.* (interrogative), *imp.* (imperative), or *exc.* (exclamatory). Write the correct punctuation mark at the end.

__________ 30. Do you know what the two middle verses of the Bible are

__________ 31. Turn to Psalm 103:1, 2

__________ 32. These verses have a significant message for their central location

__________ 33. How important it is for us to bless the Lord

__________ 34. You should memorize these verses and their reference

(5 points)

D. Label each sentence *N* for natural word order, *I* for inverted word order, or *M* for mixed word order. Then rewrite the sentence in a different word order. Use correct punctuation.

______ 35. Out in the orchard stands a gnarled apple tree. ______________________________

____

______ 36. This tree has produced a fine crop for many years. ______________________________

____

______ 37. During last year's drought, we were able to irrigate the orchard. ____________________

____

______ 38. There are several bushels of fine red apples on its branches now. ____________________

____

____

(8 points)

E. Label each sentence *S* (simple), *Cd* (compound), or *Cx* (complex).

______ 39. The Bible contains much practical advice for youth.

______ 40. Because many young people prefer their own plans, God commands them to remember their Creator in their youth.

______ 41. Paul wrote and encouraged Timothy, who was a young church leader.

______ 42. Young people can choose wrong habits and attitudes, or they can develop a solid character.

(4 points)

F. Label the underlined clauses *ind.* for independent, *adj.* for adjective, or *adv.* for adverb.

__________ 43. The Sermon on the Mount, which Matthew records in detail, opens with the Beatitudes.

__________ 44. This notable sermon describes the life that Jesus wants His followers to live in this world.

__________ 45. Although such a life is not natural to man, it is possible through the grace of God.

__________ 46. Those who consistently follow Christ's teachings are building their lives on the Rock.

__________ 47. Because Jesus taught with authority, the people were astonished at His words.

(5 points)

G. These sentences include simple, compound, and complex sentences. Diagram the skeletons and complements of all the clauses.

48. The sun is the center of the solar system, and the planets orbit it.

49. The sun is one star in the vast universe.

50. The earth is the planet that God designed for the existence of life.

51. Because no other planet can support life, man inhabits only Earth.

52. We worship our great God, who created this temporary habitation for man.

(27 points)

H. Read the paragraphs below, and do these exercises.

53. Write *chronological*, *spatial*, or *importance* to identify the type of sentence order that is used.

_________________ a. Paragraph 1 _________________ b. Paragraph 2

54. Write the numbers that identify these sentences.

_____ a. The topic sentence of Paragraph 1.

_____ b. The topic sentence of Paragraph 2.

_____ c. The sentence that mars the unity of Paragraph 2.

55. Copy the words in Paragraph 1 that illustrate the following things.

_____________ _____________ a. Repetition of key words (two synonyms).

_____________ _____________ b. Pronoun reference (two pronouns).

Paragraph 1:

[1]The monarch butterfly is a marvel of creative design. [2]Out front it has two antennae, delicately sensing the air to help the monarch find the nectar of its favorite flowers. [3]Behind the antennae are two eyes with six thousand lenses each, seeming to bulge out of proportion to the rest of its head. [4]In the entire creation, these eyes are among the best for sensitivity to motion—as you can readily believe if you ever try to catch a monarch. [5]This butterfly, like all insects, has six legs. [6]But the monarch's legs serve the unusual function of tasting its food! [7]Overspreading most of the monarch's body are its four beautiful wings of orange and black. [8]Each wing is covered with millions of overlapping scales. [9]If you touch a wing, these tiny scales rub off and look like powder on your finger.

Paragraph 2:

[1]As autumn starts bringing colder weather, lonely monarch butterflies start winging their way south. [2]Later these monarchs may congregate in large groups, especially at difficult crossings. [3]After a journey of as much as two thousand miles, they reach their winter homes in Florida, California, or Mexico. [4]The monarchs find their way back to their summer homes when spring arrives. [5]Of all the species in the butterfly world, only the monarch and a few others migrate south for the winter.

(7 points)

Total points: 85

Building Securely

Chapter 3 Test

Score ____________

Name ____ **Date** ________________________

A. Circle *T* if the statement is true or *F* if it is false.

T F 1. A good paragraph developed by giving steps has each step numbered.

T F 2. For musical terms ending with *o,* you should add *-es* for the plural forms.

T F 3. In writing a plural form, you should change a final *y* to *i* if it comes after a consonant.

T F 4. A good paragraph developed by using examples might have only two examples if enough details are given about each.

T F 5. A paragraph developed by giving a definition is like a brief story.

T F 6. A paragraph can be developed by using more than one method.

(6 points)

B. In the first blank, write *C* or *A* to tell whether the noun is concrete or abstract. In the second blank, write *M, F, N,* or *C* to tell whether its gender is masculine, feminine, neuter, or common.

_____ _____ 7. road

_____ _____ 8. Michael

_____ _____ 9. honesty

_____ _____ 10. sheep

_____ _____ 11. seamstress

_____ _____ 12. teacher

_____ _____ 13. contentment

_____ _____ 14. hen

(8 points)

C. Change each word in parentheses to a noun by using a noun-forming suffix.

15. The (lead) of our tour thanked us for our (cooperate).

____________________ ____________________

16. The (identify) of God's people is marked by their godly (separate).

____________________ ____________________

17. The Christian's (fortify) is in his (depend) on the Lord.

____________________ ____________________

(6 points)

D. Write *X* before the underlined words that are used as nouns.

18. If we do not _____ praise the Lord daily, we cannot live to His _____ praise.

19. After I ______ box these sheets and this ______ cover, I want you to ______ cover the ______ box with gift-wrapping.

(6 points)

E. Correct the capitalization errors by crossing out each incorrect letter and writing the correct letter above it.

20. The lord told abram to leave ur and go to a new Land.
21. We bought a Baker's Wood Stove in marysville.
22. The Pioneers left the east in a Covered Wagon they named *prairie wings*.
23. The cedar lake Mennonite Church should be finished by july, and the new School should be ready by Fall.

(9 points)

F. Write the plural form of each noun. For numbers 32–35, use the foreign spellings.

24. motto ______________
25. journey ______________
26. louse ______________
27. city ______________
28. shelf ______________
29. soprano ______________
30. sister-in-law ______________
31. eyetooth ______________
32. oasis ______________
33. index ______________
34. vertebra ______________
35. fungus ______________

(12 points)

G. Rewrite these expressions, using possessive forms. If a possessive form should not normally be used, write *correct*. Show joint ownership for numbers 40 and 41, and separate ownership for numbers 42 and 43.

36. the papers of the children ______________________________
37. the hands of the clock ______________________________
38. the comb of the rooster ______________________________
39. the time of three weeks ______________________________
40. the rabbits of Lloyd and George ______________________________
41. the idea of Marjorie and Helen ______________________________
42. the answers of Leah and Eugene ______________________________
43. the pencils of Larry and Dorothy ______________________________

(8 points)

H. Each sentence contains one verbal phrase or noun clause. Underline it, and in the blank write *G, I,* or *C* to identify it as a gerund phrase, an infinitive phrase, or a noun clause.

______ 44. Mother was wondering if Father had finished the chores.

______ 45. To leave by 5:30 is still our goal.

______ 46. Whatever you can do will be appreciated.

______ 47. Mother's only job was combing the girls' hair.

(4 points)

I. Underline the substantives in these sentences. Do not underline separately the substantives within phrases or clauses.

48. The boys are hoeing the beans in the garden, and you should help them.

49. Raising produce for the market requires hard work from the whole family.

50. We enjoy working together, and we know that God blesses hard work.

51. Our market, Mary, is at Avery Square in Smithsburg.

(8 points)

J. Diagram the skeletons and complements of the clauses in these sentences. Include verbals and their complements and the introductory words of noun clauses.

52. Speaking kindly about others shows a thoughtful attitude.

53. The student's responsibility is to respect his teacher.

54. Lucinda said that she enjoys poetry.

55. How she can write such good poetry is a mystery to me.

(19 points)

K. Write *X* before the better paragraph in each pair.

56.

_____ a. God's Word is absolutely sure. Nothing in the Bible can fail or change. Jesus said that not one jot or tittle would pass from the Law until all was fulfilled. And everything in the Bible will certainly be fulfilled, for God's Word is forever settled in heaven. God's Word is completely worthy of our full confidence.

_____ b. God's Word is absolutely sure. Many of its prophecies have already come to pass, and we know that all the rest will also be fulfilled. Without fail, Bible promises have encouraged and inspired those who have claimed them. The principles taught in the Bible will never fail if they are applied diligently. God's Word is completely worthy of our full confidence.

57.

_____ a. The force of atmospheric pressure can be shown by a simple demonstration. You will need an empty metal can with a tight-fitting cap, some water, and a hot plate or stove. With the cap off the can, heat a small amount of water in the can. After the water is hot, take the can off the burner, put on the cap, and pour cold water over it. As the steam in the can condenses, a partial vacuum is produced. Atmospheric pressure on the outside of the can is so great that it will crush the can.

_____ b. The force of atmospheric pressure can be shown by a simple demonstration. First, get an empty metal can with a tight-fitting cap, some water, and a hot plate or stove. Second, put a small amount of water into the can and heat it with the cap off the can. Third, take the can off the burner and put on the cap. Fourth, pour cold water over the can so that the steam condenses and a partial vacuum is produced. Atmospheric pressure on the outside of the can is so great that it will crush the can.

(2 points)

Total points: 88

Building Securely

Chapter 4 Test

Score ____________

Name ______________________________ **Date** ______________

A. Circle *T* if the statement is true or *F* if it is false.

T F 1. In a sentence about two past actions or conditions, the one that occurred first is often expressed in the past perfect tense.

T F 2. In a sentence about two future actions or conditions, the one that occurs second is often expressed in the future perfect tense.

T F 3. In English grammar, *perfect* means "precise."

T F 4. The emphatic form of a verb can be used only in the present and past tenses.

T F 5. In both topical and sentence outlines, each item should begin with a capital letter.

T F 6. In both topical and sentence outlines, each item should end with a period.

(6 points)

B. Match the terms to the descriptions by writing the letters of the correct choices in the blanks.

a. present perfect
b. past perfect
c. future perfect
d. transitive verb
e. intransitive complete verb
f. intransitive linking verb

_____ 7. Indicates action that was completed by a certain time in the past.

_____ 8. Indicates action that began in the past and is now completed.

_____ 9. Indicates action that will be completed by a certain time in the future.

_____ 10. Helping verb *have* or *has* is used.

_____ 11. Helping verbs *shall have* or *will have* are used.

_____ 12. Helping verb *had* is used.

_____ 13. An action verb that does not pass action.

_____ 14. A form of *be* or some other verb that does not express action.

_____ 15. An action verb that passes action to a receiver.

_____ 16. A verb that acts like an equal sign between the subject and the predicate nominative.

(10 points)

C. Write the missing principal parts. Use a helping verb with the third part.

First (Present)	Second (Past)	Third (Past Participle)
17. drag	____________	________________
18. go	____________	________________
19. think	____________	________________
20. do	____________	________________
21. come	____________	________________
22. burst	____________	________________

(12 points)

D. Underline each verb or verb phrase. In the blank, write the letter showing the tense of the verb.

a. present
b. past
c. future
d. present perfect
e. past perfect
f. future perfect

_____ 23. The righteous man regards the life of his beast.

_____ 24. By noon we had cleaned the whole downstairs.

_____ 25. We shall surely finish the upstairs this afternoon.

_____ 26. By tomorrow at this time, Grandfather's will have arrived.

_____ 27. They have never visited us at our new place yet.

_____ 28. A heifer has broken through the fence.

_____ 29. The heavy rain washed some deep gullies in the garden.

_____ 30. Will the carpenters finish the roof today?

(8 points)

E. Write the correct verb or verb phrase in each blank, as indicated in parentheses.

31. Carl ________________ his books and papers too often. (present tense of *forget*)

32. My brother ________________ our class tomorrow. (future tense, progressive form of *teach*)

33. Kevin ________________ to third base before the outfielder threw the ball. (past perfect tense of *run*)

34. I ________________ the assignment in my assignment book. (past tense, emphatic form of *write*)

(4 points)

F. In the blank, write the word that receives the action of the verb.

____________ 35. The cherries have been eaten by the birds.

_______________ 36. Father bought two goats at the auction today.

_______________ 37. Aden made a beautiful box for Mother's recipe cards.

(3 points)

G. In each sentence, underline the two words that are linked by the verb.

38. Saul was the first king of Israel.

39. This hot stew will taste good to the tired men.

40. The corn has not grown tall during this dry weather.

(3 points)

H. Label the patterns of these sentences.

Pattern 1: intransitive complete verb
Pattern 2: transitive verb; action passed to direct object
Pattern 3: transitive verb; action passed to subject
Pattern 4: intransitive linking verb

______ 41. For seventy years the Israelites had been captives.

______ 42. Sister Mabel has been writing to us regularly.

______ 43. Many inspiring lessons are taken from David's life.

______ 44. Harvey did bring his butterfly collection to school.

______ 45. The rainbow soon became brilliant.

(5 points)

I. Diagram the skeletons, complements, and verb modifiers of these sentences.

46. Seth is proofreading his story.

47. Louella has been a good helper.

48. The airplane was tossed violently by the strong winds.

49. Sally gave us an account of her day with the Smiths.

(14 points)

J. Each line on this outline has one mistake. Write it correctly as a topical outline.

Nehemiah—a Man of Action

I. The source of his Strength
  A. prayer
    1. when he heard disturbing news
    2. He needed to answer the king
    3. When he faced opposition.
  b. Concern for the welfare of God's people
  C. He knew God's Word.
  D. He was consecrated.
  E. Faith and Trust in God
    1. seen in his many prayers
    2. Seen in his confidence in the hand of God.
II. What the secret of his strength was

Nehemiah—a Man of Action

(12 points)

Total points: 77

Building Securely

Chapter 5 Test

Score ____________

Name ____ **Date** ________________________

A. Circle *T* if the statement is true or *F* if it is false.

T F 1. If two singular subjects are joined by *and,* the verb should be singular.

T F 2. A verb in the passive voice passes its action to the subject.

T F 3. The passive voice is suitable when there is no clear doer of an action.

T F 4. In a friendly letter, the greeting should be followed by a colon.

T F 5. In a business letter, the inside address should come before the heading.

T F 6. A thank-you note or other social note should have the same five parts as a friendly letter.

(6 points)

B. Underline the correct words.

7. Everyone in the nation of Israel (is, are) safely over the Jordan River.
8. (There's, There are) two men spying on Jericho.
9. Rahab (don't, doesn't) want to be destroyed with Jericho.
10. Rahab, as well as those with her, (was, were) delivered.
11. Everybody who was not behind the scarlet line (have, has) been destroyed.
12. A flock of geese (pass, passes) overhead on its way south.
13. With modern medication, smallpox (have, has) been wiped out.
14. My small scissors (have, has) fallen out of my purse.
15. (Do, Does) these clouds foretell snow?
16. Our herd of cows (is, are) contentedly chewing their cuds.

(10 points)

C. Choose the correct verb for each sentence, and write it in the proper form.

______________ 17. Samuel thought Eli had called, and he (raise, rise) quickly.

______________ 18. Samuel returned to his bed and (lay, lie) down again.

______________ 19. Eli was (set, sit) on a bench when the news came.

______________ 20. Because Eli had (let, leave) his sons persist in evil, his household was severely punished.

_____________ 21. Our hopes of rain have (raise, rise) with the cloudy skies.

_____________ 22. We must hurry and smooth the concrete before it (set, sit).

_____________ 23. (Can, May) we take a break afterward?

(7 points)

D. Write the correct verb for each sentence.

_____________ 24. Pharaoh and his army were drownded in the Red Sea.

_____________ 25. God's people have often been attackted viciously.

_____________ 26. Solomon's temple costed an enormous amount of money.

_____________ 27. The dedication service must of greatly inspired the godly.

_____________ 28. Olen had broke his arm once before.

_____________ 29. Brendon drug the heavy crate across the barn floor.

_____________ 30. Dallas throwed ten bales of straw down to bed the heifers.

_____________ 31. Barry has brung the pitchforks to spread the straw.

_____________ 32. The blister on my finger has bursted.

_____________ 33. Mother has tooken a treat out for the men in the field.

(10 points)

E. Write whether the verbs in these sentences are *active* or *passive.*

_____________ 34. A person's heart is revealed by his words and actions.

_____________ 35. Love always seeks the welfare of others.

_____________ 36. Father led the family in a prayer of thanksgiving.

_____________ 37. Our parents' guidance should be appreciated deeply.

_____________ 38. Important training for life is being given daily.

(5 points)

F. The passive voice is used in each sentence below. Before each one, write the letter of the statement which correctly describes that sentence.

a. The active voice would be more effective.
b. There is no clear doer of the action.
c. There is a good reason not to name the doer.

_____ 39. These pillow tops were crocheted by a friend.

_____ 40. Bronze is made from copper and tin.

______ 41. A story was told by our teacher.

______ 42. A page has been torn out of Leanne's new book.

(4 points)

G. Read the following friendly letter. In the numbered blanks, list three mistakes that you see in the letter.

Route 2, Box 215
Rutherfordton, NC 28139

Dear Sidney,

Well, I haven't written to you for a while, so I thought I would write again.

Last week we went to the Philadelphia zoo. That was a lot of fun!

Have you gotten your rabbit hutches built already? Do you have rabbits too? I'm eager to see your setup. Maybe I'll be able to buy some rabbits from you and start raising some here. I'll ask Father about that.

Our cantaloupes are almost ready. That means a lot of work for the next several weeks. We've been selling a lot of sweet corn already.

I hope we can come and see you sometime soon.

Your cousin
Joseph

43. ______________________________

44. ______________________________

45. ______________________________

(3 points)

H. Read the following business letter. In the numbered blanks, list three mistakes that you see in the letter.

Route 1, Box 93
Croghan, NY 13327
March 3, 20—

Dear Sirs,

I would like some information about the products you sell. Send whatever you can immediately.

Respectfully yours,
Jonas King

46. ______________________________

47. ______________________________

48. ______________________________

(3 points)

Total points: 48

Building Securely

Chapter 6 Test

Score ____________

Name ____ **Date** ________________________

A. Circle *T* if the statement is true or *F* if it is false.

T F 1. Only personal pronouns in the third person have different forms according to gender.

T F 2. Apostrophes are used in spelling personal pronouns in the possessive case.

T F 3. A compound personal pronoun is used reflexively when it is a direct object naming the same person or thing as the subject.

T F 4. The interrogative and the relative pronouns are identical except in their use within a sentence.

T F 5. When you prepare note cards for an oral report, you may write two or three items of information on each card.

T F 6. The pronouns *who* and *whom* should refer only to persons, and the pronoun *which* should refer to anything except persons.

(6 points)

B. Write whether each pair of pronouns is different in person (*P*), number (*N*), case (*C*), or gender (*G*).

_____ 7. I, we

_____ 8. I, me

_____ 9. theirs, ours

_____ 10. me, him

_____ 11. him, her

_____ 12. they, them

(6 points)

C. Write a pronoun for each of the following descriptions.

__________ 13. second person, objective case

__________ 14. first person, singular, nominative case

__________ 15. third person, plural, objective case

__________ 16. third person, singular, possessive case, masculine gender

__________ 17. first person, plural, objective case

__________ 18. third person, singular, nominative case, feminine gender

(6 points)

D. Write *N* or *O* to tell whether each underlined pronoun is in the nominative or objective case.

_____ 19. Moses cast down his rod, and <u>it</u> became a serpent.

_____ 20. Never let hardships discourage <u>you</u>.

______ 21. The person taking this test is <u>you</u>.

______ 22. When you receive advice, you should benefit from <u>it</u>.

(4 points)

E. Underline the correct choices in parentheses.

23. The gifted poet and storywriter kept (her, their) note pad handy to jot down ideas.
24. The tenor singers, Brent and (he, him), are struggling with this new song.
25. For Alice and (I, me), this was an enjoyable day.
26. Father told (we, us) boys to clean out the calf hutches.
27. Either Julia or Judy had (her, their) quilt block here today.
28. (We, Us) young people must learn to practice good habits.
29. The most surprised persons must have been you and (I, me).
30. Mother gave Charlotte and (she, her) clear directions.
31. The secretary and treasurer gave (his report, their reports).
32. The secretary and the treasurer gave (his report, their reports).

(10 points)

F. Rewrite these sentences to make the pronouns clear and correct.

33. When Harry raced with Dale, he tripped and sprained his ankle. ______________________________

____

34. Michael told Raymond that his answer was right. ______________________________

____

35. Father said that me and you may walk back to the creek. ______________________________

____

(3 points)

G. Cross out the wrong word in each sentence. If another word should be used instead, write the correct word in the blank.

______________ 36. Because Moses sinned, he hisself lost the right to enter Canaan.

______________ 37. The sons of Eli made theirselves vile.

______________ 38. Them are the cedars of Lebanon.

______________ 39. Nobody volunteered for that there job.

_______________ 40. We should discipline ourself to do what we know is right.

_______________ 41. Jonathan and myself will come to help you.

(6 points)

H. Underline the correct choices in parentheses.

42. Everybody (have, has) been created to glorify God.

43. Nobody can fill this place in only (his, their) own strength.

44. None of God's Word (is, are) ever outdated or false.

45. None of God's promises (is, are) vain.

46. Few of the angels (have, has) names known to man.

47. Each of the patriarchs had (his, their) special trials in life.

(6 points)

I. Underline the relative pronoun in each sentence, and draw an arrow from it to its antecedent.

48. Job, whose life was greatly changed in one day, trusted God.

49. Satan, who falsely accused Job, could not destroy that faith.

50. The unwavering faith that Job had in God was the key to his steadfastness.

51. These troubles, with which Satan intended to destroy Job, only strengthened his faith.

(8 points)

J. Label the underlined pronouns *P* for personal, *CP* for compound personal, *D* for demonstrative, *ID* for indefinite, *IR* for interrogative, or *R* for relative.

_____ 52. Find <u>yourselves</u> seats while dinner is prepared.

_____ 53. Was <u>that</u> an interesting school trip?

_____ 54. This is the day <u>that</u> the Lord has made.

_____ 55. We must use <u>our</u> abilities to serve the Lord.

_____ 56. <u>Both</u> of the ideas are worthy of consideration.

_____ 57. I did not ask for <u>these</u>.

_____ 58. <u>Whom</u> did God choose to be the first king of Israel?

_____ 59. Saul, <u>whom</u> God chose as the first king, soon fell into disobedience.

(8 points)

K. Write the following information on the note cards. The notes are taken for the topic "Coal, an Important Fuel."

— hard anthracite best coal for fuel (*Investigating God's Orderly World,* Book 1, page 226)
— appears to be formed from mainly plant material, fossilized under pressure (*Biology for Christian Schools,* page 187)

(4 points)

L. Write *X* before the two best headings under which the information in Part K and below should be organized.

— soft, brown lignite burns poorly (*Investigating God's Orderly World,* Book 1, page 226)
— soft but blacker bituminous is a better fuel (*Investigating God's Orderly World,* Book 1, page 226)
— not known to be forming in natural world today (*Biology for Christian Schools,* page 187)

_____ 60. The Discovery of Coal

_____ 61. The Formation of Coal

_____ 62. The Kinds of Coal

_____ 63. The Uses of Coal

(2 points)
Total points: 69

Building Securely

Chapter 7 Test

Score ____________

Name ________________________________ **Date** ____________________

A. Circle *T* if the statement is true or *F* if it is false.

T F 1. Descriptive adjectives answer the questions *which, whose,* and *how many.*

T F 2. A participle is a verb form used as an adjective.

T F 3. If two descriptive adjectives are used together, they are often separated by a comma.

T F 4. Restrictive clauses should be set off by commas.

T F 5. *Less* should be used with singular nouns, and *fewer* with plural nouns.

T F 6. *Them* may be used as a pronoun and an adjective.

(6 points)

B. Write the letter of the correct term to match each description. Some letters may be used more than once.

a. metaphor
b. personification
c. simile
d. hyperbole

_____ 7. A figurative exaggeration for emphasis.

_____ 8. A figurative comparison using *like* or *as.*

_____ 9. A figurative comparison not using *like* or *as.*

_____ 10. Giving human characteristics to a thing or quality.

_____ 11. Saying that one thing is another thing, or using literal terms to describe something that happened only in a figurative sense.

e. appositive position
f. attributive position
g. predicate position

_____ 12. An adjective following a linking verb, modifying the subject.

_____ 13. An adjective coming right after the word it modifies.

_____ 14. An adjective coming just before the word it modifies.

_____ 15. Adjectives often coming in pairs and set off by commas.

(9 points)

C. Underline the seven adjectives in these sentences. Above each, write *D* for descriptive or *L* for limiting.

16. One Indian family attended the worship service.

17. Joseph's coat of many colors must have been beautiful.

(7 points)

D. Cross out each word that should not be used, and write any correction above it. If words are missing, use a caret (∧) to show where they belong, and write the words in the space above the sentence.

18. The Garden of Eden must have been beautifuller than we can imagine.

19. Before the Flood, people grew more older than they do today.

20. According to the lesson, your answer is more correct than mine.

21. Although I felt ill yesterday, I feel even iller today.

22. Both girls explained the game, but Darlene's explanation was clearest.

23. Leon has littler experience with driving tractors than Ira has.

24. How do you like this here story?

25. A dishonest liar loses the confidence of others.

26. The chickens laid less eggs today than yesterday.

27. The loud, noisy children needed something worthwhile to do.

28. Eileen copied them recipes from her cousin's collection.

29. Do you know what kind of a squash this is?

(12 points)

E. Underline each adjective phrase. In the blank, write whether the phrase is prepositional (*prep.*), participial (*part.*), or infinitive (*inf.*).

__________ 30. Moses and Joshua, nearing the camp, heard a strange sound.

__________ 31. The people in the camp were singing and shouting.

__________ 32. Aaron's willingness to please the people had led to great sin.

__________ 33. Seeing the golden calf, Moses knew that the people had broken their commitment

__________ to serve the Lord.

(5 points)

F. Add the missing commas to these sentences. For those given in pairs, write *R* or *N* in the blank to tell which sentence has a restrictive clause and which has a nonrestrictive clause.

34. The long low boat sped down the river muddy and swollen.

______ 35. a. The man who owned the boat was taking a load of produce to market.

______ b. Philadelphia which was his destination was a bustling market town.

_____ 36. a. The Ten Commandments which God gave to Moses are found in Exodus 20.

_____ b. The teachings that Jesus gave represent even higher standards.

(8 points)

G. Underline each adjective phrase or clause that is misplaced, and draw an arrow from it to the place where it belongs.

37. The lame man asked for alms seeing Peter and John.

38. The new book is out on the porch that Aunt Faye sent us.

39. This shirt needs to be mended with a big hole.

(3 points)

H. Diagram these sentences.

40. Lightning, striking a nearby tree, killed several cattle.

41. Mother, who prepared this nourishing breakfast, deserves our hearty thanks.

42. Barry is the one whom I tagged.

43. The books within these boxes are the ones to take along.

(23 points)

I. Write whether each sentence contains a metaphor (*M*), a simile (*S*), a hyperbole (*H*), or personification (*P*).

______ 44. Aunt Velma carries the glow of sunshine wherever she goes.

______ 45. The trees whispered together in the breeze, and the flowers nodded to each other.

______ 46. Do not make a mountain out of a molehill.

______ 47. Clyde's thoughtless words stung like a whip.

______ 48. The children, as nervous as mice watched by a cat, waited for Father to return.

(5 points)

J. Write a more exact noun or a more expressive verb for each underlined expression.

49. Use this <u>white thing</u> to write the problem on the board. ______________________

50. The thunder <u>made a loud noise</u>, and we jumped. ______________________

51. Three black <u>animals</u> escaped up the tree as Rover ______________________

<u>came after</u> them.______________________

(4 points)

Total points: 82

Building Securely

Chapter 8 Test

Score ____________

Name ______________________________ **Date** ______________

A. Circle *T* if the statement is true or *F* if it is false.

T F 1. *Badly* and *well* are always adverbs.

T F 2. An adverb clause at the beginning of a sentence must be followed by a comma.

T F 3. An adverb clause begins with a subordinating conjunction.

T F 4. A book report should not reveal the theme and main events of the story.

T F 5. In a book report, you should avoid giving your own evaluation of the book.

T F 6. A book report should briefly describe the setting of the story.

T F 7. For giving an explanation of a process, the most common order of development is chronological order.

T F 8. In an oral explanation, the introduction is generally of little importance.

(8 points)

B. Underline the eight single-word adverbs, and draw an arrow from each one to the word it modifies.

9. Worldly wisdom too often ignores the true wisdom of God's Word.

10. Man never finds true wisdom unless he lays aside his own will.

11. Man quickly became exceedingly wicked in the early history of the world.

12. One holy family drew near to the Lord and lived faithfully.

(8 points)

C. Underline the eight adverb phrases, and draw an arrow from each one to the word or words it modifies.

13. Wise men from the East came into Jerusalem and inquired about the newborn King.

14. They were sent by Herod to Bethlehem.

15. In a dream, God warned the wise men about Herod's evil intentions.

16. They departed into their own country by a different way.

(8 points)

D. Underline the six adverb clauses, and draw an arrow from each one to the word or words it modifies.

17. When the wise men did not return to him, Herod was filled with anger.

18. Jesus was safe from Herod's wrath because God had warned Joseph to flee to Egypt.

19. After Herod died, Joseph returned to the land of Israel as an angel had directed him.

20. Since Joseph paid close attention to God, God could lead him where He wanted him to go.

(6 points)

E. Label each underlined word, phrase, or clause by writing *adj.* or *adv.* above it.

21. That car with the flat tire must be moved off the busy road.

22. The man at the far end of the bench has traveled far today.

23. Do not drive too fast on this rough road.

24. The reason that we are late will be understood when you hear our story.

25. The lonely man sat down under the stately trees.

(10 points)

F. In each blank, write the correct form of the adverb in parentheses.

26. Laura works (well) ______________ and talks (quietly) ______________ than her sister.

27. The large lion behaved (wildly) ______________ than the lioness did.

28. Of the two neighbor boys, Ronald acted (badly) ______________.

29. Towns on the flat prairies can be spotted (far) ______________ away than in these rolling hills.

30. Of the four hikers, Albert worried the (little) ______________ about getting lost.

(6 points)

G. Cross out the incorrect words. If other words should be used instead, write them in the blanks.

______________ 31. Elijah must have been sort of depressed as he lay under the juniper tree.

______________ 32. Pilate couldn't find no fault in Jesus.

______________ 33. Rehoboam was real harsh with the people.

______________ 34. A fruitful branch must be connected up with the vine.

______________ 35. Jesus always answered His enemies too good for them to trap Him.

______________ 36. Simon brought no water for Jesus to wash up His feet.

______________ 37. The woman of Sychar couldn't hardly believe that a Jew would speak to her.

______________ 38. Jews usually treated Samaritans very bad.

______________ 39. As Jesus spoke, the woman of Sychar sought after the living water.

______________ 40. She was kind of startled that Jesus knew so much about her.

(10 points)

H. Diagram these sentences.

41. Our recently purchased typewriter operates very quietly.

42. The cows are walking slowly across the road to the meadow.

43. Three young goats are eating grass at the edge of the woods.

44. After Father marked the rows, we planted the seeds.

45. The grass has become greener than we had expected.

(24 points)
Total points: 80

Building Securely

Chapter 9 Test

Score ____________

Name ________________________________ **Date** ____________________

A. Write the letter of the correct term to match each description. In each set, one letter must be used twice.

_____ 1. Word that shows strong feeling or emotion.

_____ 2. Connecting words that work in a pair.

_____ 3. Connecting word that introduces a phrase.

_____ 4. Any one of these words: *and, but, or, since, when, because.*

_____ 5. Connecting word that shows relationship between its object and some other word.

_____ 6. Word like *and,* which always joins sentence parts of parallel structure and function.

_____ 7. Connecting word that joins an adverb clause to an independent clause.

_____ 8. Connects two independent clauses and is preceded by a semicolon.

a. conjunction
b. conjunctive adverb
c. coordinating conjunction
d. correlative conjunction
e. interjection
f. preposition
g. subordinating conjunction

_____ 9. Regular pattern of accented and unaccented syllables.

_____ 10. Repetition of beginning consonant sounds.

_____ 11. Repetition of matching sounds at ends of lines.

_____ 12. Repetition of similar vowel sounds in accented syllables.

_____ 13. Repetition of similar or opposite ideas.

_____ 14. Pattern shown with small letters such as *abcb.*

_____ 15. Accented syllable and the unaccented syllable or syllables associated with it.

_____ 16. Use of a word having an imitative sound.

h. alliteration
i. assonance
j. onomatopoeia
k. parallelism
l. poetic foot
m. rhyme
n. rhythm

_____ 17. Two unaccented syllables followed by one accented syllable.

_____ 18. One accented syllable followed by one unaccented syllable.

_____ 19. One unaccented syllable followed by one accented syllable.

_____ 20. One accented syllable followed by two unaccented syllables.

_____ 21. The most common rhythm in English poetry.

o. anapestic
p. dactylic
q. iambic
r. trochaic

(21 points)

B. Underline each prepositional phrase, and above it write *adj.* for adjective phrase or *adv.* for adverb phrase. If one phrase is part of a longer phrase, underline it twice and label both phrases clearly.

22. Before His suffering and death, Jesus went to the Garden to pray.

23. His sleeping disciples could not understand His agony of spirit.

24. As Peter stood in the group around the fire, one person recognized him by his speech.

25. Peter denied his Lord because of his fear.

(7 points)

C. Underline each conjunction or conjunctive adverb, and label it *CC* for coordinating conjunction, *SC* for subordinating conjunction, or *CA* for conjunctive adverb. Be sure to include all the parts of a correlative conjunction.

26. A diligent attitude and a disciplined mind are key ingredients for successful study.

27. We must strive for the best; however, we must be content with the abilities that God has given us.

28. Youthful habits influence a person's life; therefore, you should develop good habits now.

29. As a person grows older, habits become harder to change.

30. All habits work either for the good or for the bad.

(5 points)

D. Underline each interjection. Place a comma or an exclamation point after each one, and capitalize the following word if necessary.

31. Whew that car almost ran off the road.

32. Rocks this farm is almost covered with them.

33. Oh now I understand this problem.

(6 points)

E. Cross out each mistake in word usage, and write any correction above it.

34. Our garden is in back of the house.

35. The sugar peas will soon be over with for this spring.

36. What kind of a tomato stalk is that?

37. Its leaves look a bit different than the leaves of the others.

38. Insects have been bothering most of the plants accept the tomatoes.

39. The salesman parked his car besides the barn.

40. Did you see that bullfrog leap in the pond?

41. Mother divided the remaining cake between us four boys.

42. Father gave this job to you and I, so let's get busy.

(9 points)

F. Underline the correct words in parentheses.

43. No doubt, my great-grandfather worked much harder than (I, me).

44. Since Sharon is handicapped, my parents must help her more than (I, me).

45. The cattle are bawling (as if, like) they are out of hay.

(3 points)

G. Above each underlined word or phrase, write what part of speech it is.

46. The Bible is a guiding light, showing the right way to the godly.

47. Godly people cling to the right, for evil ruins those who fall into it.

48. For those airplanes that fly through the air, a partial vacuum is necessary.

49. Crash! Mother's treasured dish lies in ruins because of my carelessness.

50. Lois will come in and vacuum the remains off the floor.

51. The will to do right should be guiding our reactions in difficulties.

52. Because Grandfather took a kindly interest in our activities, we treasured his visits.

53. Act kindly toward the elderly; they are often weaker than we are.

(34 points)

H. In the blank before each stanza, write which pattern of rhythm it has. In the blanks after the lines, show the rhyming pattern.

54. ____________________

The snow is like a blanket that ______
God spreads across the land, ______
Where wheat and oats and barley sleep, ______
Awaiting spring's command. ______

55. ____________________

The Assyrian came down like the wolf on the fold, ______
And his cohorts were gleaming in purple and gold; ______

And the sheen of their spears was like stars on the sea, ______

When the blue wave rolls nightly on deep Galilee. ______

56. ________________

When at last I near the shore, ______

And the fearful breakers roar ______

'Twixt me and the peaceful rest, ______

Then, while leaning on Thy breast, ______

May I hear Thee say to me, ______

"Fear not, I will pilot thee." ______

57. ________________

Wisdom is bidding in still and sweet voice, ______

Bidding each one to his soul's solemn choice: ______

Wisdom or folly—which way will you take? ______

Wisdom brings true godly honor and joy, ______

Folly the soul of a man will destroy; ______

Wisdom or folly—this choice all must make. ______

58. Draw one line under the simile and two lines under the example of personification in number 54.
59. Underline the words that show alliteration in number 55.
60. Underline the word that shows onomatopoeia in number 56.
61. Underline the words that show assonance in number 57.

(13 points)

I. Write whether the parallelism in each verse is similar (*S*) or opposite (*O*).

______ 62. "But he that sinneth against me wrongeth his own soul: all they that hate me love death" (Proverbs 8:36).

______ 63. "Reprove not a scorner, lest he hate thee: rebuke a wise man, and he will love thee" (Proverbs 9:8).

______ 64. "In the way of righteousness is life; and in the pathway thereof there is no death" (Proverbs 12:28).

(3 points)

Total points: 101

Building Securely

Chapter 10 Test

Score ____________

Name ______________________________ **Date** ____________________

A. Circle *T* if the statement is true or *F* if it is false.

T F 1. A restrictive adjective clause should be set off with commas.

T F 2. A question mark is placed outside the quotation marks if the whole sentence is a question but the quotation is not.

T F 3. A period is always placed outside the quotation marks.

T F 4. If a verb is followed by several direct objects in a list, a colon should be placed after the verb.

T F 5. A semicolon may be used between two independent clauses even if no conjunction is used.

T F 6. To show what is italicized in print, you underline in writing.

T F 7. A story conflict should be introduced in the middle of the story.

T F 8. The climax should be described in the last several sentences of the story.

T F 9. Dialogue in a story should consist of formal language and complete sentences.

T F 10. A good storywriter avoids using many linking verbs and passive voice verbs.

(10 points)

B. Cross out each error in capitalization, and write the correct letter above it.

11. At the store, mother bought some Mueller's Noodles on a special sale.

12. The Springville Shoe store is owned by Alfred Bender, sr.

13. The Yosemite national park is on the West slope of the Sierra Nevada.

14. Thanksgiving day always comes on a thursday.

15. My Father enjoyed Math when he was a student in School.

16. Every morning, o lord, thou wilt hear our prayers.

17. We read some Verses from the word of God.

(16 points)

C. Add the missing commas and end marks.

18. Jericho which lies northeast of Jerusalem was the hometown of Zacchaeus

19. Did you know Marie that Jericho is eight hundred feet below sea level

20. Jericho is less than twenty miles from Jerusalem yet Jerusalem is about twenty-five hundred feet above sea level

21. What a steep climb that must be

22. A cool refreshing breeze made a pleasant day for hoeing in the garden digging postholes and picking up stones in the field.

23. Because we wanted to surprise Father we worked hard in fact at all three jobs.

24. Eric was born on July 15 1970 at Jefferson City Missouri.

(14 points)

D. Add quotation marks and other related punctuation. Show any correction of capitalization as you did in Part B. Do not put quotation marks around a sentence that has no explanatory words.

25. In the Bible began Brother Herbert we find the source of all truth.

26. In His prayer, Jesus said Thy Word is truth he continued.

27. How sad that many people say Truth is whatever man discovers

28. Pilate asked what is truth

(12 points)

E. Add underlining or quotation marks where they are needed.

29. Father had read Four Centuries of Dutch Mennonitism from the book Glimpses of Mennonite History and Doctrine.

30. At the close of the service, we sang Now the Day Is Over.

31. Use Strong's Exhaustive Concordance to find the verse.

32. Did you read Long Days for Leah in the Christian Pathway?

(6 points)

F. Add the missing colons and semicolons. You will need to replace some commas with these marks.

33. Ralph Waldo Emerson made this statement, "The reward of a thing well done is to have done it."

34. We drove through Washington, the Evergreen State, Oregon, the Beaver State, and California, the Golden State.

35. Our neighbors have lived in the following states, Vermont, Ohio, Iowa, Mississippi, and Florida.

36. Floyd says that it's exciting to live in so many different places, I'm glad to stay here on our farm.

37. I would be willing to move if God calls us somewhere else, however, their father moves to find the highest paying jobs he can.

(5 points)

G. Add apostrophes, hyphens, and underlining where they are needed.

38. I dont have any great grandparents living anymore.

39. Long ago, ss within words looked much like fs.

40. The word shew is pronounced the same as show.

41. Mr. Getz still has twenty two desks with self contained lamps.

42. The word parallel has only one set of double ls.

43. Somebodys cows are loose, but they arent ours.

44. The Flying Eagle, our neighbors small airplane, was lost during the sudden tem pest last week.

(15 points)

H. Improve each sentence so that the dialogue sounds more natural.

45. "There is a beautiful rainbow out here," said Dennis.

46. "Where is the rainbow?" said Lynette.

47. "The rainbow is over the meadow," said Dennis. "Let us go and tell Mother."

45. ______________________________

46. ______________________________

47. ______________________________

____

(8 points)

I. Rewrite these sentences to include more lively action verbs that show rather than merely tell.

48. It was a bitterly cold day. ______________________________

____

49. These books have all been read by me. ______________________________

____

(4 points)

Total points: 90

Building Securely

Chapter 11 Test

Score ____________

Name ____ **Date** ________________________

A. Circle *T* if the statement is true or *F* if it is false.

T F 1. The etymology of a word shows its different forms, such as plurals and principal parts.

T F 2. Generally the beginning of a sentence receives the greatest emphasis.

T F 3. One good way to write an emphatic sentence is to separate a verb phrase with a lengthy interruptive phrase.

T F 4. Prefixes usually change the part of speech of a word, and suffixes change the meaning of a word.

T F 5. The index of an encyclopedia gives more details on finding information than do the cross-references.

T F 6. Encyclopedias give information on many subjects in greater detail than most books.

T F 7. The Old Testament was written in Greek.

T F 8. Careful speakers and writers avoid using words that the dictionary labels *nonstandard* or *illiterate*.

(8 points)

B. Write the letter of the correct term to match each description. You may use a letter more than once.

a. atlas	d. dictionary	g. topical Bible	j. homographs
b. Bible dictionary	e. encyclopedia	h. antonyms	k. homophones
c. concordance	f. thesaurus	i. heteronyms	l. synonyms

______ 9. A book of synonyms.

______ 10. A book of Bible words and their references.

______ 11. A book of words, showing pronunciations, meanings, and other information.

______ 12. A book of maps.

______ 13. Volumes of information containing articles on a wide range of subjects.

______ 14. A book of Bible subjects, with verses pertaining to each subject.

______ 15. A book of information on Bible words, places, people, and customs.

______ 16. A book that may have dictionaries of the Hebrew and Greek words from which English words in the Bible were translated.

______ 17. Words that are spelled and pronounced alike but have different origins and meanings.

______ 18. Words with similar meanings.

______ 19. Words that are spelled alike but pronounced differently.

______ 20. Words with opposite meanings.

______ 21. Words that are pronounced alike but spelled differently.

(13 points)

C. All the following words have the root *gress,* which means "to go or step." In the blanks below, write the words that match the definitions.

aggressive	progress	regression
digress	progression	transgressor

____________ 22. To go forward.

____________ 23. One who steps across (a boundary line).

____________ 24. The action of going back.

____________ 25. To go away from (a topic of discussion).

(4 points)

D. Use suffixes to change the following words to the parts of speech indicated.

________________ 26. hard (n.)

________________ 27. permanent (n.)

________________ 28. persecute (n.)

________________ 29. sail (n.)

________________ 30. final (v.)

________________ 31. glory (adj.)

________________ 32. color (adj.)

________________ 33. absence (adj.)

________________ 34. marvel (adj.)

________________ 35. active (v.)

(10 points)

E. Make each sentence more effective by using the active voice, using a direct quotation, improving the parallelism, making the pronoun reference clear, removing wordiness, or moving a modifier to a better position.

36. Roxanne must choose to bake brownies or cooking custard. ____________________

____

37. Mother said that Lori must bake some bread. ____________________

____

38. The cleaning will be done by Joyce and Esther this time. ____________________

____

39. When we hit that sharp rock, the tire almost went flat immediately. ____________________

____

40. Father told the neighbor man that his wood supply should last all winter. ____________________

____

41. After the starting bell rang, Brother Noah announces the opening song. ______________________

____

____

42. To expostulate is when you object earnestly but kindly. ______________________

____

43. A ruffed grouse seemed to suddenly appear from nowhere. ______________________

____

44. A grouse's sudden, abrupt takeoff into flight often surprises and startles people. ______________________

____

____

(9 points)

F. Rewrite the following paragraph, making the changes indicated to give greater sentence variety.

45. Change sentence *a* to an interrogative sentence.
46. Combine sentences *b* and *c* into a compound sentence.
47. Change sentence *d* so that the dependent clause comes first.
48. Combine sentences *e* and *f* into a complex sentence.
49. Change sentence *g* to inverted word order.
50. Change sentence *h* to an exclamatory sentence.

[a]The Amazon River is the largest river system in the world. [b]This huge river is only the second longest. [c]It carries the greatest volume of water. [d]Over one thousand tributaries join the mighty Amazon before it completes its four-thousand-mile journey to the Atlantic. [e]The river drains an area of 2.5 million square miles. [f]This is over two-thirds of the area of the entire United States. [g]Its fresh water flows far out into the Atlantic Ocean. [h]The Amazon is an amazing river indeed.

____

____

____

____

____

____

____

____

____

(6 points)

Total points: 50

Building Securely

Final Test

Score ____________

Name ______________________________ **Date** ______________

A. Circle *T* if the statement is true or *F* if it is false.

T F 1. If a verb is in a perfect tense, a form of *have* is always used as a helping verb.

T F 2. Modifying words, like adjectives and adverbs, are substantives.

T F 3. A character sketch should give one main impression about a person.

T F 4. A paragraph explaining a process should be developed in the order of importance.

T F 5. In addition to the parts of a friendly letter, a business letter has a heading.

T F 6. A paragraph has coherence when the ideas flow smoothly from one sentence to the next.

T F 7. A topic sentence may be found anywhere within a paragraph.

T F 8. The story conflict should be introduced early in the story.

T F 9. The climax of a story should be found in the middle of the story.

T F 10. One good way to make dialogue sound natural is to use expressions like "he don't" and "we seen."

(10 points)

B. Before each sentence, write the abbreviation for the part of speech that the underlined word is.

______ 11. We surveyed the damage <u>after</u> the storm was over.

______ 12. <u>After</u> the next town, we will see no service stations for a while.

______ 13. The older boys ran, and the younger ones had trouble following <u>after</u>.

______ 14. The calves in this pen look well, but <u>those</u> look rather sick.

______ 15. <u>Those</u> paragraphs were well developed.

______ 16. <u>Rich</u>! Solomon must have been richer than we can imagine.

______ 17. The <u>rich</u> are not always the happiest.

______ 18. God's blessing is <u>rich</u> even though earthly riches may be scarce.

______ 19. The <u>singing</u> birds sounded very cheerful.

______ 20. <u>Singing</u> can be a good way to encourage yourself.

______ 21. The students are singing the new song quite well.

______ 22. We practiced the song quite often, for it was difficult to learn.

______ 23. We sang it for the closing song in devotions this morning.

(13 points)

C. In each blank, write what sentence part the underlined word is. Use the following abbreviations.

S—subject
V—verb
DO—direct object
IO—indirect object
PN—predicate nominative
PA—predicate adjective
DA—noun of direct address
AP—appositive

______ 24. You will grow strong in character if you love the truth.

______ 25. Guard carefully your attitudes about right and wrong.

______ 26. Give your parents the respect that God calls you to give.

______ 27. Your present attitudes will become an important key to your future character.

______ 28. In the midst of daily temptations, you must determine to be faithful.

______ 29. Do you know if Mother is resting, Twila?

______ 30. Midnight, the cat lying on the step, catches many mice.

______ 31. Do you plant string beans every year?

______ 32. The train's whistle sounded loud and clear.

______ 33. A passerby saw the fire and sounded an alarm.

(10 points)

D. In the first blank, write *S* for simple, *Cd* for compound, or *Cx* for complex to identify the structure of the sentence. In the second blank, write *N* for natural, *I* for inverted, or *M* for mixed to identify the word order of the sentence.

______ ______ 34. The way of the world promises pleasure, but it brings misery.

______ ______ 35. When the Jews fell into idolatry, were they better off?

______ ______ 36. Gehazi coveted this world's goods and suffered for it.

______ ______ 37. How great was his punishment!

______ ______ 38. Follow the Lord, and love not the world.

(10 points)

E. In each blank, write *prep.* for prepositional, *part.* for participial, *ger.* for gerund, or *inf.* for infinitive to identify the underlined phrase.

__________ 39. Peter, misjudging himself, said that he would die for Jesus.

__________ 40. The self-confident person fails to seek God's help.

__________ 41. He trusts rather in the strength of his own heart.

__________ 42. Trusting one's own self is a sure formula for failure.

__________ 43. We should pray to the Lord every day.

(5 points)

F. In the first blank, write *D* or *I* to tell whether the underlined clause is dependent or independent. If the clause is dependent, write the abbreviation for noun (*n.*), adjective (*adj.*), or adverb (*adv.*) in the second blank.

_____ _______ 44. Although it is May already, the weather has been quite cool.

_____ _______ 45. A large ocean liner was passing under the Bay Bridge while we were driving over it.

_____ _______ 46. We saw what the hailstorm did to your corn.

_____ _______ 47. A beautiful spring day dawned, but I was sick in bed.

_____ _______ 48. I am returning the books that you loaned me last month.

(5 points)

G. Fill in the blanks of this chart. For the starred words, use the foreign plural spellings.

Singular	Singular Possessive	Plural	Plural Possessive
49. monkey	__________	__________	__________
50. brother-in-law	__________	__________	__________
51. calf	__________	__________	__________
52. prince	__________	__________	__________
53. man	__________	__________	__________
54. sheep	__________	__________	__________
55. *larva	__________	__________	__________
56. *fungus	__________	__________	__________
57. *crisis		__________	
58. *vertex		__________	

(10 points)

H. Identify the person (*1, 2, 3*), number (*S, P*), case (*N, O, P*), and gender (*M, F, N, C*) of each underlined pronoun.

	Person	Number	Case	Gender
59. The Bible guides us.	______	______	______	______
60. He sent a Saviour.	______	______	______	______
61. Sue helped her nicely.	______	______	______	______
62. Children, are you ready?	______	______	______	______
63. Look at its torn pages!	______	______	______	______

(10 points)

I. Underline the correct words.

64. Abraham gave them, Hagar and (he, him), food and water for their journey.

65. Isaac's two sons, Jacob and (he, him), were quite different.

66. When the man asked for Mr. Shrock, Father replied, "I am (he, him)."

67. May (we, us) students eat lunch beside the creek at noon?

68. The secretary and treasurer gave (his answer, their answers).

(5 points)

J. In each blank, write the tense of the underlined verb.

__________________ 69. The Lord willing, we shall have arrived home before evening.

__________________ 70. The Lord certainly did bless us with safe traveling.

__________________ 71. Too often we have forgotten to thank Him for His blessings.

__________________ 72. We shall thank Him before we leave the car.

__________________ 73. We are seeking His daily blessing on our lives.

__________________ 74. We had seen four accidents before we left Illinois.

(6 points)

K. From Part J, copy the verbs that fit these descriptions.

__________________ 75. a verb in a progressive form

__________________ 76. a verb in an emphatic form

(2 points)

L. Write numbers in the blanks to identify the sentence patterns.

Pattern 1: intransitive complete verb
Pattern 2: transitive verb, active voice
Pattern 3: transitive verb, passive voice
Pattern 4: intransitive linking verb

______ 77. "My cup runneth over."

______ 78. "The word of the Lord is right."

______ 79. "All his works are done in truth."

______ 80. "I will bless the Lord at all times."

(4 points)

M. Underline the better words.

81. (There's, There are) many examples of sowing and reaping in the Bible.
82. Mother's scissors (have, has) been misplaced.
83. Either Esther or Miriam (was, were) using them this morning.
84. Father said we (can, may) fly our kite after chores.
85. We should (let, leave) the younger ones choose first.
86. Chicken pox (is, are) caused by the same virus as shingles.
87. After the heavy rains, the creek (raised, rose) over its banks.
88. Don't gather the eggs in this nest; this hen is (setting, sitting).
89. Grandfather has been (laying, lying) in bed for two weeks.
90. The bags of feed (have, has) been delivered.
91. The balloon (burst, busted) with a loud pop.
92. Paula has (went, gone) along with Mother to the store.
93. Henry (tagged, tug) Clyde between second and third base.
94. The ice cream has (froze, frozen) hard by now.
95. Please (raise, rise) the shade to let the sun shine in.

(15 points)

N. In the first blank, write *D* for descriptive or *L* for limiting to describe the underlined adjectives. In the second blank, write *AT* for attributive, *AP* for appositive, or *PR* for predicate.

_____ _____ 96. A <u>difficult</u> task awaited Kenneth.

_____ _____ 97. <u>Two</u> calf pens needed to be cleaned out.

_____ _____ 98. The morning air felt <u>fresh</u> and crisp.

_____ _____ 99. The task, difficult but <u>necessary</u>, was soon finished.

_____ _____ 100. The work was made easier by <u>his</u> good attitude toward it.

(10 points)

O. Write the comparative and superlative degrees of these adjectives and adverbs.

101. helpful _______________ _______________

102. well _______________ _______________

103. holy _______________ _______________

104. pleasant _______________ _______________

105. great _______________ _______________

106. far _______________ _______________

(6 points)

P. Cross out each word that should not be used, and write any correction above it.

107. Them ten spies who brought an evil report lacked faith in God.

108. There were less spies who saw the Lord than who saw the difficulties.

109. But these here two spies, Joshua and Caleb, were richly rewarded by God.

110. Both boys gave correct answers, but Leon's was most satisfactory.

111. Do you know what kind of a bird whistles like that?

112. How long can the men continue on battling this blazing fire?

113. Mr. Morgan sounded kind of upset when we invited him to come to church.

114. We will divide these chores between the five boys.

115. Be careful not to fall off of the ladder.

116. The cows went in the barn for shelter from the rainstorm.

(10 points)

Q. Cross out each capitalization error, and write the letter correctly above it. Not every item has an error.

117. a warm summer day
118. a quiz in American History
119. God and his holy angels
120. the song "Now the day is over"
121. our Whirlpool Refrigerator
122. the Cedar Ridge feed and seed
123. during the middle ages
124. a State in the west

(8 points)

R. Add the two missing punctuation marks to each sentence. Underlining one or more words counts as one mark.

125. Your diligence today, my friend will certainly pay off in the future
126. Did David who was a man after God's own heart, ever make any mistakes
127. Yes he did sin grievously several times but he always repented afterward.
128. What Bible character said "I have played the fool?
129. Although he recognized his folly he did not sincerely repent indeed, he finally took his own life.
130. "You are to memorize the poem 'One by One, stated Brother John.
131. "Youll find the poem in the book Poems for Memorization," he continued.
132. My great grandfather Bauman was respected as a man of self control.
133. There's a large number of ands in that paragraph.
134. The following books make up the Pentateuch Genesis, Exodus, Leviticus, Numbers and Deuteronomy.

(10 points)

S. Write the letter of the correct term to match each description. A letter may be used more than once.

_____ 135. The repetition of thoughts.

_____ 136. The repetition of beginning consonant sounds.

_____ 137. The repetition of similar vowel sounds.

_____ 138. The matching of sounds at the ends of lines.

_____ 139. The use of words having imitative sounds.

_____ 140. The regular pattern of accented and unaccented syllables.

_____ 141. A device more common in Bible poetry than in English poetry.

_____ 142. An accented syllable and the unaccented syllable or syllables associated with it.

a. alliteration
b. assonance
c. onomatopoeia
d. parallelism
e. poetic foot
f. rhyme
g. rhythm

(8 points)

T. Read this paragraph, and do the exercises below.

[a]You have a four-chambered heart that constantly circulates blood through your body. [b]First, the right ventricle pumps the blood to the lungs, where it is supplied with oxygen. [c]From the lungs the blood returns to the left atrium and empties into the left ventricle. [d]Then the left ventricle pumps the oxygen-rich blood to the various parts of the body. [e]Sometimes germs enter the blood from these body parts. [f]Having delivered its oxygen, the blood returns to the right atrium, flows into the right ventricle, and is pumped to the lungs again. [g]In this way the blood follows a definite path as it flows through the body.

______ 143. Write the letter of the topic sentence.

______ 144. Write the letter of the sentence that mars the unity.

______ 145. Write whether the paragraph is developed by (a) adding details, (b) giving steps, (c) using examples, (d) telling an incident, or (e) giving a definition.

(3 points)

U. Each starred line on this partial outline contains a mistake. Write the outline correctly on the lines below.

The Process of Digestion

I. In the mouth
  *A. teeth
    *1. Break food into small pieces
  B. Saliva
  *1. Moistens food
    *2. Starches are changed into sugars.
*II. The stomach

The Process of Digestion

____

____

____

____

____

____

____

(5 points)

Total points: 165